FRANK LLOYD WRIGHT'S
SETH PETERSON COTTAGE

FRANK LLOYD WRIGHT'S
SETH PETERSON COTTAGE

RESCUING A LOST MASTERWORK

JOHN EIFLER   ■ ■ ■   KRISTIN VISSER

Prairie Oak Press
Madison, Wisconsin

Second edition, first printing
Copyright © 1997 by the Wisconsin Trust for Historic Preservation
Second edition copyright © 1999 by Prairie Oak Press

Prairie Oak Press
821 Prospect Place
Madison, WI 53703

Designed by Flying Fish Graphics, Blue Mounds, Wisconsin
Printed in the United States of America on acid-free paper by BookCrafters, Chelsea, Michigan

Library of Congress Cataloging-in Publication Data

Eifler, John.
    Frank Lloyd Wright's Seth Peterson Cottage : rescuing a lost masterwork / John Eifler and Kristin Visser. — 1st ed.
        p.   cm.
        Includes index.
        ISBN 1-879483-62-9 (acid-free paper)
        1. Seth Peterson Cottage (Wis.) 2. Wright, Frank Lloyd, 1867-1959—criticism and interpretation. 3. Usonian houses—Wisconsin—Sauk County—Conservation and restoration. 4. Peterson, Seth, 1936-1960—Homes and haunts—Wisconsin—Sauk County.
I. Visser, Kristin, 1949-1998 . II. Title.
NA7235.W6E38 1997
728'.37'0977576—dc21   96-49980
                                                            CIP

Funding for this book provided by the Jeffris Family Foundation, Janesville, Wisconsin, and by the Graham Foundation for Advanced Studies in the Fine Arts, Chicago, Illinois.

This book is dedicated to Audrey Laatsch,
who never wavered in her vision of what the cottage could be.

■   ■   ■

CONTENTS

ACKNOWLEDGMENTS

We first want to thank the many volunteers and the contractors who worked on the cottage rehabilitation. Their spectacularly successful efforts provide the basis for this book.

Invaluable assistance in preparation of this book was provided by members of the Seth Peterson Cottage Conservancy Board of Directors, especially Audrey Laatsch and Bill Martinelli, who helped find photos and who carefully reviewed the manuscript for errors and omissions. Thanks also to board members Mark Vladick, who made available his videotaped interview with Tom Casey, and Tim Heggland, who reviewed the manuscript. Board members Jan Aslaksen and Trudy Wright provided us with documents from the conservancy archives.

Special thanks to Seth's sister Carolyn Royster, who talked to us about Seth and his efforts to build the cottage, and to Seth's close friend Bert Goderstad, who provided insight into Seth's life and gave us copies of Seth's letters to him. Bruce Brooks Pfeiffer, Oscar Munoz, Margo Stipe, and other staff at the Taliesin Archives were most helpful in tracking down Peterson-related documents and drawings in the archives, as was Kristin Hammer, librarian at the Getty Center for the History of Art and the Humanities, where many of the Taliesin Archive documents are stored on microfiche. We also want to thank Rob O'Riordan who assisted with research and manuscript preparation.

We also wish to thank Tom Jeffris, president of the Jeffris Family Foundation, who wanted the story of the cottage rehabilitation told to a wide audience, and who provided a grant for research and production of this book. Likewise, our appreciation to the Graham Foundation for Advanced Studies in the Fine Arts which provided additional financial support for this project.

INTRODUCTION

The little cottage designed by Frank Lloyd Wright for Seth Peterson was never considered one of Wright's most important projects. In fact, very little was ever published about the building until the rehabilitation project was underway. But during the process of planning the rehabilitation of the cottage, it became clear that this overlooked work was, in fact, a significant architectural statement, a building that was certainly worthy of preservation. The manner in which the building was rehabilitated is also significant, in that a unique group of individuals from the private and public sectors joined together to save the cottage from ruin.

The Seth Peterson Cottage is now open to the public, and can be rented by anyone, provided they respect the building. Located deep in a heavily forested state park, the cottage provides a unique opportunity for individuals to enjoy living in a Frank Lloyd Wright house, if only for a few days. Some guests have returned as often as four times since its dedication in 1992, and plan to return in the future. The board of directors that assumed curatorial responsibilities for the building continues to marvel at the overwhelming interest in the cottage. Historical buildings are usually operated by cash-poor not-for-profit entities, but in the case of the cottage the board is now in the unique position of changing the color of the financial ink from red to black.

In this book we have focused primarily on the practical aspects of building rehabilitation. The *process* of preserving buildings is the issue, and we hope to provide new insight into the philosophy of restoring buildings through the preservation of the cottage and the development of this book. We hope that the story of the cottage rehabilitation will be of interest to other organizations managing historic buildings and will continue to inspire the ongoing restoration of America's architectural treasures, no matter how grand or small.

John Eifler
Kristin Visser
October, 1996

PART I

THE COTTAGE

■ ■ ■

The Seth Peterson Cottage as it appeared in the 1960s.

◪ PART I • THE COTTAGE

The Seth Peterson Cottage was designed in 1958 and represents Frank Lloyd Wright's final Wisconsin commission. At only 880 square feet, the cottage is one of Wright's smallest homes and was designed as a variation on Wright's Usonian theme. The Peterson Cottage design is the Usonian home stripped to its essence: tiny kitchen, a small bath, a bedroom, and a combined living/dining space, all surrounding the massive fireplace. The cottage lacks a carport, a hallway, and a primary entryway. The concept of unobstructed spatial flow is prevalent throughout the cottage, as evidenced by the lack of interior doors. There are only two—one on the bathroom and another on the utility closet. Because Peterson was on a tight budget, Wright scaled down the utilitarian Usonian plan to produce what Taliesin architect Tom Casey called a one-room space, a building contained "under one ceiling."

Despite the cottage's small size, Wright's chief assistant, William Wesley Peters, claimed the structure contained "more architecture per square foot than any building Wright ever built." The building feels surprisingly spacious due to the sloped shed roof sheltering the living/dining space. The sloped roof rises from six feet eight inches to twelve feet to allow an abundance of natural light through the window wall which wraps around three sides of the living/dining space. The kitchen is a typical Usonian galley, open to the dining and living area. The kitchen, like that in other Usonians, is two stories high, topped by a flat roof with a skylight, giving it a spacious feel even though it is quite tiny. (The bathroom and a storage loft above, along with the fireplace masonry, are also part of this two-story element.) The bedroom, by contrast, with its low ceiling and band of narrow windows, feels cozy and cocoon-like.

Built primarily of local sandstone, Douglas fir-faced plywood, cedar shingles, and glass, the cottage sits on the edge of a bluff overlooking Mirror Lake. Viewed from below, its strong battered terrace and walls, along with the soaring roof and large window wall, give the building a monumentality that is surprising to find in such a small structure. Unlike most lakeside cottages which are sited to maximize views, the Seth Peterson Cottage is oriented almost sideways to the lake. This gives a southwestern orientation to the large window wall, which allows the warming rays of the sun to penetrate the cottage during the winter, while the large cantilevered roof overhang protects the interior space from the hot

COTTAGE   FOR   MR   SETH   C.   PETERSON
MIRROR   LAKE,   WISCONSIN
FRANK   LLOYD   WRIGHT   ·ARCHITECT

summer sun. The terrace is located on the northwest side of the cottage, and provides a striking view of the lake and summer sunsets. Finally, the bedroom, with its narrow band of windows and large roof overhang, is located on the northeast corner, shielded from direct sun but allowing for early morning light in the summer.

The Seth Peterson Cottage is one of the last examples of Wright's Usonian homes, a housing type that was first realized with the construction of the first Herbert Jacobs House in Madison, Wisconsin, designed in 1936. The Usonian home was Wright's personal solution to America's need for moderate-cost housing. Wright believed, "In our country the chief obstacle to any real solution of the moderate-cost house problem is the fact that our people do not really know how to live. They imagine their idiosyncrasies to be their 'tastes,' their prejudices to be their predilections, and their ignorance to

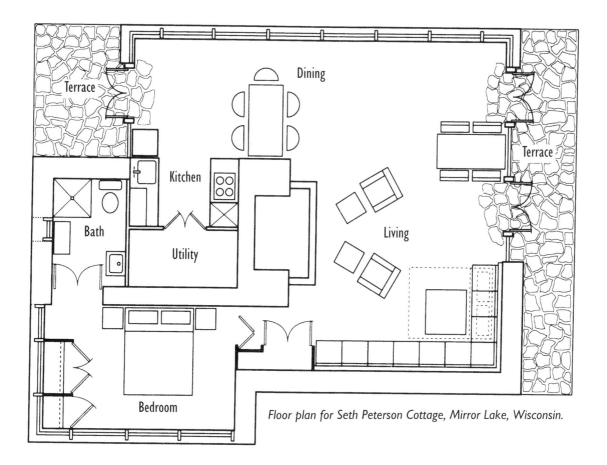

Floor plan for Seth Peterson Cottage, Mirror Lake, Wisconsin.

be virtue—where any beauty of living is concerned." In the Jacobs I House, Wright established the Usonian home as a specific type characterized by:

1. Elimination of the basement, except for a fuel and heater spot.
2. Elimination of the attic and, therefore, elimination of the visible roof.
3. No painting or plastering. All materials to be sealed with clear oils and waxes.
4. No garage—a carport will do.

5. No radiators or heating grilles, heat to be provided by a radiant floor hot-water heating system.
6. Floor plans designed according to a planning module, usually a multiple of four feet.

The first Usonian houses were built from relatively inexpensive materials such as plywood and boards with concrete floors. The use of brick was limited to chimneys and selected walls. Nearly all of the first Usonians were designed with flat roofs. In time, Wright further developed the concept by experimenting with alternative building materials and various plan and roof types.

Wright's use of the dramatic shed roof similar to the one on the Seth Peterson Cottage began to appear in his designs as early as 1936 in a design for the living room of a large home in Marquette,

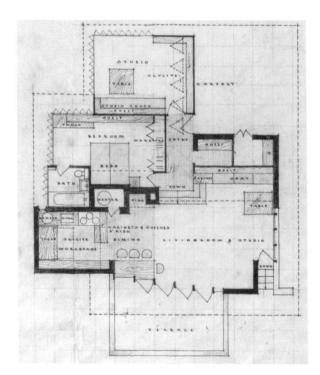

Floor plan for the Berta Hamilton project.

Michigan, and reappeared in other Wright designs of the 1940s and 1950s. The design origins of the Seth Peterson Cottage can be directly traced to an unbuilt 1947 design for a small summer cottage Wright did for Berta Hamilton in Brookline, Vermont. Like the Seth Peterson Cottage, the Hamilton project gathers the living and dining areas under a sloping roof with a large window wall. A terrace, enclosed by a low parapet wall, projects from the living area. A bedroom and studio are tucked under a flat roof behind the central fireplace. The kitchen is located to one side in a two-story masonry mass under a flat roof. Later that year, Wright proposed a two-bedroom variation of the Hamilton project to Ruth Keith, who commissioned a design for a summer cottage in Pennsylvania. Unfortunately, she also elected not to pursue construction.

Another direct link with the design of

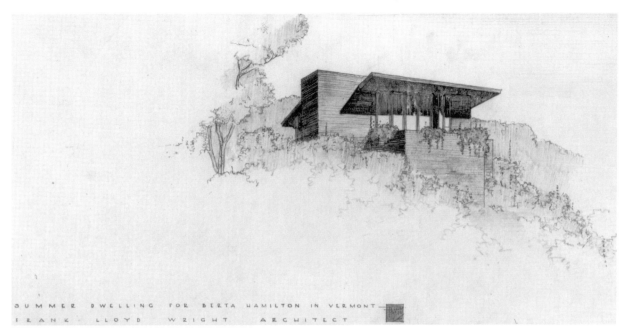

SUMMER DWELLING FOR BERTA HAMILTON IN VERMONT
FRANK LLOYD WRIGHT ARCHITECT

Architect's rendering for the Berta Hamilton project.

the Seth Peterson Cottage is the 1952 design for Archie Teater in Bliss, Idaho. Wright was never one to throw away a good plan, and in this case he conceived a small residence/studio on a diamond grid, based on the earlier Hamilton project. The design transforms the Hamilton project one step closer to the Seth Peterson Cottage by relocating the primary entry to the side of the shed roof, adjacent to the kitchen area. Once again, the combined living/dining area is located beneath a large shed roof, and the kitchen, living, and dining areas surround a massive central fireplace. A single bedroom and bath were placed behind and to one side of the fireplace.

Simultaneous with the Peterson Cottage, Wright designed a house for Don Sturmquist in Bountiful, Utah. The 1958 Sturmquist House contains many of the elements found in both the Peterson Cottage and Teater Studio. This house was conceived on a diamond grid, yet has a continuous living/dining/kitchen area radiating from a central hearth. The terrace, enclosed by a low parapet wall, projects from the exterior facade of the living area. The utility and bath rooms were placed behind the kitchen.

An extended bedroom wing, placed behind the bathroom, makes this house considerably larger than the Peterson Cottage. By removing the bedroom wing and increasing interior angles from 60 degrees to 90 degrees, Wright could have produced a very near cousin of the Peterson Cottage.

There is little documentary detail about the commission, design, and construction of the Seth Peterson Cottage. Many of the principal characters are deceased and others have uncertain memories of the events surrounding the building of the cottage.

Seth Peterson (1936-1960) was born and grew up in Black Earth, Wisconsin, a small community located halfway between Madison and Spring Green. Even as a boy, Peterson was fascinated with the work of Frank Lloyd Wright. He and his best friend, Bert Goderstad, used to take the train to Oak Park, Illinois, to stroll through town looking at Wright designs. After he graduated from high school in 1954, Peterson applied for admission to the Taliesin Fellowship as an apprentice, but couldn't afford the required $1500 annual tuition. He applied again in 1956 and early 1957, but was again turned away with the explanation that he must have the $1500 tuition and that the fellowship had no room for new apprentices.

After graduation from high school, Peterson took a job as an IBM computer operator for the state Department of Motor Vehicles. In 1957 he joined the Army because of his desire to gain more computer training. After basic and advanced training, he was posted to Belgium and France. Peterson suffered a severe asthma attack and was given a medical discharge after only about a year of Army service.

Upon his return, Peterson became friends with a woman who owned land on Mirror Lake in nearby Sauk County, about 50 miles north of Madison. In July 1958 he bought a small cottage and several adjoining lots totaling 1.18 acres on the lake along with a driveway easement for a total cost of $7,500. He moved into the cottage and, having resumed his job with the state, commuted from Mirror Lake

Seth Peterson's 1954 high school graduation photo.

to Madison. This cottage was destroyed by a fire that was apparently caused by a faulty space heater or electrical connection only a few months after Peterson moved in.

Neither the Taliesin archives nor Peterson's personal correspondence indicates when Peterson first approached Frank Lloyd Wright for a cottage design, but family members believe it was after the original cottage on his Mirror Lake property burned down. However, then-apprentice Tom Casey, who was assigned to oversee cottage construction, recalled that Wright and apprentice John Howe worked on the design during the summer of 1958 while the fellowship was in Wisconsin.

At this point in Wright's career apprentices were given the responsibility of developing rough initial sketches after consultation with Wright on a design concept. Wright would periodically check on the progress of the design and order changes until a proposed plan could be presented to the client for approval. In the late 1950s, Wright's workload and his advanced age prevented him from visiting most sites, and he relied on topographic maps and photographs to get a feel for the terrain, the sun patterns, and vegetation. He used this approach with the cottage design. Even though Mirror Lake is only about 40 miles from Taliesin, Wright never visited the site.

The drawings evidently took time to complete, as a note from Peterson appended to a letter to Taliesin in December 1958 asks about progress on the construction drawings for his cottage. The drawings must have been completed in early 1959, as Peterson made two payments totaling $600 to Taliesin against the total $1350 design fee (9% of the estimated $15,000 construction budget), in April 1959. Thus, it is very likely that the final drawings were completed before Wright's death that same month.

In July 1959, Peterson and his parents took out a $12,000

During construction, 1959.

construction mortgage at the Baraboo Federal Savings and Loan. Peterson had contracted with local Lake Delton builder Macky Adams to build the cottage. Adams and Tom Casey found a quarry in Rock Springs, just 20 miles away, which could supply a buff-colored sandstone consistent with Wright's intentions. An August 1959 letter from Peterson to Bert Goderstad indicates that cottage construction was progressing and Peterson and his then-fiancée planned to occupy the cottage in November. (Peterson later broke off the engagement.) A series of photographs taken during the summer and fall of 1959 by an unknown photographer documents the progress of cottage construction. The building shell appears to have been completed by October 1959.

Another Peterson letter in January 1960 notes that the cottage is "nearly completed," lacking only the furnace and plumbing fixtures. Peterson notes that he and his fiancée have spent weekends at the cottage, using a space heater and the fireplace to stay warm. The reason for the apparent slow pace of construction isn't clear, although contractor Macky Adams and two subcontractors did file liens against the property in October 1959 and March and April 1960 that totaled more than $8,900. Although difficult to substantiate, it appears that Peterson was having financial troubles brought on by costs exceeding the original $15,000 construction budget and the associated construction loan. This is evidenced not only by liens, but also by the physical changes to the design which were accomplished to reduce costs. For example, the in-floor radiant heating system was scrapped in favor of a less costly forced-air system, the approach drive to the cottage was shortened, and three-inch steel hinges were used on all the doors and windows instead of the solid brass piano hinges specified by Wright. Finally, insect screens were evidently not provided, although they are detailed on the

Masonry under construction, 1959.

After the masonry was completed, work on the roof began, 1959.

Interior nearing completion, 1959.

construction drawings.

Seth Peterson took his own life on April 17, 1960, at his parents' home in Black Earth, only two months shy of his 24th birthday. He left no note or any indication as to why he took an action that was so unexpected by those around him. The cottage was essentially complete, lacking only a few interior details. Friends and relatives believe that he was distraught over financial problems stemming from the cottage. Because of the lack of records, the total cost of the cottage is unknown. If the liens reflect the overrun on the original $15,000 estimate, the construction cost would total about $24,000. Contractor Macky Adams recalled that his cost estimate was $26,000. A 1964 appraisal completed when the state was negotiating to buy the property estimated the original cost of the building at $34,875. Whatever the final number, it was considerably higher than the price of an average house in 1960. In spite of Wright's hopes, the Seth Peterson Cottage reinforces the opinion held by many that Usonian houses never turned out to be the moderately priced housing for the middle class that he envisioned.

After Peterson's death, the cottage sat empty until April 1962, when it was purchased for $15,000 by Lillian Pritchard, a Milwaukee widow, as a residence for her son Owen. He moved in, erected a six-foot-high chain link fence around the property, and added several outbuildings, including a storage shed/guest cabin, and kennels for his pet Afghan hounds. He also toyed with the idea of enlarging the cottage and commissioned the Taliesin Fellowship to design a large bedroom/studio addition which would have extended behind the existing bedroom. The Taliesin proposal included a greatly enlarged terrace and a swimming pool. Pritchard was unable to finance the addition, however, and dropped the plans.

Living room of Owen Pritchard with view of Mirror Lake.

View from living room into bedroom, mid-1960s.

The cottage was offered for sale by the Pritchards a few years later, but no buyers surfaced. In September 1966 the state purchased the cottage from Lillian Pritchard for $38,400 for inclusion in the newly created Mirror Lake State Park. The state wanted the land on which the cottage stood for inclusion in the park. In most cases an unwanted building such as the cottage, if it could not be used for park purposes, would be sold for salvage or for intact removal—or it would be razed. In the course of negotiating with Mrs. Pritchard (it took two years to agree on a sale price), state officials realized that the cottage was historically and architecturally important because it was a Wright design. In their correspondence several officials discussed options for its use, including a nature center, a visitors center, and a "Wright memorial," presumably a museum. In the end, park officials were unable to find a park-related

Pritchard's terrace with view of Mirror Lake at right.

use for the cottage, which is more than a mile away from the park headquarters and main park developments. Unwilling to destroy a Wright building, park managers finally boarded up the cottage and left it alone in the woods.

PART 2

RESCUING A LOST MASTERWORK

■ ■ ■

The cottage interior in 1989.

■ PART 2 • RESCUING A LOST MASTERWORK

Nearly everyone living on Mirror Lake was aware of the seemingly abandoned little cottage. It had stood boarded up for over twenty years, and lake residents had developed a growing concern as the years of neglect and weather took their toll. Members of the Mirror Lake Association, a group of homeowners on the lake, felt that a building designed by Frank Lloyd Wright was too important to be left in such a deteriorated condition. They decided to see what could be done. A committee of association members led by Audrey Laatsch met with state park officials in the fall of 1988 to discuss the possibility of a group taking over the cottage to restore it and use it as a vacation rental cottage. Coincidentally, at the same time Paul Hayes, a *Milwaukee Journal* reporter, wrote an article about the cottage for the newspaper's Sunday magazine. The arti-cle publicized the decrepit state of the building and the need to preserve it. It was through this article that John Eifler first heard of the cottage.

In 1989, the Seth Peterson Cottage was seriously deteriorated and had been boarded up.

John was one of about 50 people who attended a public meeting in Wisconsin Dells in February 1989 that was a result of the earlier meeting with park officials. Those attending included representatives of the Mirror Lake Association, the State Historical Society of Wisconsin, the Department of Natural Resources (the agency that operates the state parks and thus is responsible for the cottage), the local state legislator, and interested members of the public. The discussion at the meeting centered on how to go about restoring a building designed by a famous architect which is owned by the state and located on public land. A brief history of the building was given, followed by a lengthy discussion about how the cottage could ultimately be used to justify its repair. Examples of other historic homes used as house museums, conference centers, private offices, and hotels were cited, but these ideas were deemed impractical because of the petite size of the building. The most plausible suggestion was that the cottage could be used as a unique vacation rental. Although the meeting did not conclude with any resolution or plan of action, it did get interested people together to begin the process of preserving the cottage.

At the conclusion of the meeting, John offered his architectural services to Audrey Laatsch, who was in charge of the meeting. He suggested that a preliminary study of the building be conducted to determine the scope of work and the associated costs involved in restoring the cottage. Even though there was as yet no official cottage preservation authority or organization, Audrey accepted the offer.

Shortly thereafter, she and other members of the Mirror Lake Association, along with others who expressed interest in working on cottage restoration, did form a separate entity, the Seth Peterson Cottage Conservancy (SPCC). The goal of the not-for-profit conservancy was to rehabilitate the cottage for short-term vacation rentals to a discerning public interested in Frank Lloyd Wright. The Seth Peterson Cottage was to become the only Wright structure in which the public could experience life as one of his clients, if only for a few nights. The state, as owner of the property, appreciated the idea of a

The rear roof was rotting in several places and the bedroom ribbon windows were boarded up.

self-sustaining cottage. The SPCC proposed to assume full responsibility for managing the cottage reha-bilitation and providing for the ongoing maintenance of the property. While optimistic and enthusiastic, conservancy leaders lacked a long-range plan and money, and they had very little understanding of the alchemy necessary to turn straw into gold. What they did have was a handful of people who shared a deep-rooted commitment to realizing a vision of what the Seth Peterson Cottage could be—a living expression of Frank Lloyd Wright's architectural talent.

PROJECT PLANNING

John began by contacting Bruce Brooks Pfeiffer at the Frank Lloyd Wright Foundation for archival information concerning the cottage. Taliesin, as always, was most helpful. Additional information was obtained from the second owners of the home, the Pritchards of Milwaukee, who loaned copies of the original drawings they had obtained from Taliesin when they had considered an addition to the cot-tage. John recruited his friend Gary Kohn at Skidmore, Owings and Merrill to assist with the project, and after meeting with Audrey Laatsch and looking over the cottage, the two architects began preparing a preliminary study of the cottage assessing the condition of the building components and offering recom-mendations for restoration.

Most preservation consultants recommend that a complete historic structure report (HSR) be conducted as the first step in any preservation project. An HSR is an extensive evaluation of a building or site, and includes its history, evaluation of current conditions, programming for future use, recommen-dations for repair, and a cost estimate for the improvements. Unfortunately, the professional fees associ-ated with an HSR are difficult for most not-for-profit groups to bear. At times the cost of a thorough HSR can exceed $100,000, the funding of which can indefinitely postpone the restoration of an historic structure. Most donors are unwilling to contribute large sums of money to produce an HSR because their interest usually centers on bricks and mortar.

In addition to the high cost, it is John's experience that most HSRs are incomplete. Unanticipated conditions are nearly always uncovered during the actual construction process, leading to a re-evaluation of the recommendations contained in the original report. The need to change the course of a project at mid-stream has the potential for creating havoc, especially when the project is administered or reviewed by a public agency such as a state historic preservation office.

The roof above the bathroom and kitchen had rotted through.

The Seth Peterson Cottage experience has shown that a preliminary study, accomplished at minimal cost, is an extremely effective tool for creating excitement, and ultimately funding, to get a project underway. The preliminary study allowed all of the parties involved in the project enough time to become familiar with the building, as well as plan for how improvements might be phased and funded. Ultimately John conducted a more detailed HSR prior to completing the working drawings, but even then, the scope and cost of the study were kept to a minimum. In this way, unanticipated conditions and additional historical information could be incorporated into the final restoration construction drawings without needing to review the overall direction of the project. This approach allowed the conservancy board, the Department of Natural Resources, Department of Administration (which must approve all building and restoration projects of state agencies), and the State Historical Society time to digest the proposed improvements and costs associated with conserving the cottage.

The preliminary study concluded that the cottage was severely deteriorated and would need the following restoration work:

• Abandonment of the structure and subsequent lack of maintenance had allowed the roof to rot through in several areas. The extensive rot and improper original installation of framing members led to the conclusion that virtually all of the framing, as well as the entire roof, needed to be replaced.

• Water infiltration had essentially destroyed all the original cabinetry and the plywood ceilings, wood trim, and interior doors, requiring replacement of virtually all the interior wood finishes.

• The original window sash and fixed glazing were severely decayed and needed extensive replacement.

• All mechanical, electrical, and plumbing systems (including the well and the septic tank) were either missing or destroyed.

The sandstone chimney masonry was heavily stained but otherwise in good shape.

The report concluded that the only salvageable material consisted of the masonry walls and chimney, the vertical wooden supports, and the ornamental clerestory panels. Repairs were estimated to cost approximately $250,000.

A comparison of the size of the cottage (880 square feet) and the projected cost showed that the restoration would cost roughly $300 per square foot! It is easy to see why restoration budgets based on average per square foot costs can be misleading.

John and Audrey met with officials from the Department of Natural Resources (DNR), Department of Administration (DOA), and the State Historical Society (SHS) to review John's preliminary recommendations. (Early discussion with state preservation agencies is imperative, as it allows all parties to establish a set of goals and objectives and discuss the merits and potential shortcomings of a preservation plan.) The first order of business was a discussion of how the project would be carried out and the planned use of the cottage. In an innovative spirit of public and private cooperation, the DNR was willing to lease the cottage to the conservancy on a long-term basis so that it could be operated as a vacation rental (although the lease also stipulates that the cottage be open at least once a year for public tours).

It was clear that SHS and DOA staff objected to a number of recommendations included in the preliminary report. The Seth Peterson Cottage project was initially viewed as a restoration. The project goal from the outset was to preserve salvageable original materials and incorporate them into the project. However, SHS staff did not want the project to be termed a restoration due to the large percentage of badly deteriorated original material which needed to be replaced. They insisted that the term *rehabilitation* be used because the preservation plan called for the substitution of new replacement materials that did not exactly match the originals that were beyond repair, such as roofing material and windows. Though some conservancy board members were disappointed that the carefully planned project would not be labeled a restoration, the rehabilitation classification allowed for improvements that were considered absolutely necessary for the proposed use of the cottage.

When a decision is made to conserve and restore historic buildings, it is important to approach the restoration work with a philosophy sympathetic to the original construction and to the design intent of the original architect. To date, the firm of Eifler & Associates has restored well over a dozen buildings designed by Frank Lloyd Wright. John has found that Wright's design philosophy creates unique and complex restoration problems, both physical and philosophical in nature.

Many of Wright's buildings were designed with an extremely optimistic view of the structural capabilities of wood and concrete. His work shows a consistent attempt to minimize structure to only that which is necessary to support the building. At times it seems he deliberately challenged the laws of physics. Furthermore, buildings designed by Wright were often constructed by contractors unfamiliar with his intentions or sometimes complex structural design. The conservation of these buildings is difficult as it often entails altering or replacing the underlying structure of the building. Though Wright's work is sometimes criticized on the grounds of insufficient structure, one should keep in mind that he probably didn't design these buildings to be the "monuments" we consider them today.

A preservation project that requires partial replacement of worn building components is always a subject of debate. The Bavarians were criticized for replacing marble in some buildings in Athens in the 1800s, and more recently the government of Egypt is being scrutinized for their replacement of stone in the Sphinx. The problem is that most purists measure the success of a project by the overall retention of original construction material, or "historic fabric." The term itself is somewhat of a misnomer in that it implies that the project is a painting or a textile, which would understandably be of great concern to an art conservator. But a building exposed to the elements is much different. We have very little control over the effects of weather and atmospheric pollutants. Often, deteriorated materials need to be replaced in order to allow the historical building to remain or to maintain the original intentions of the architect.

Although retaining historic fabric is important in any restoration project, it is far more reasonable to prioritize the significance of building materials. For example, the retention of interior and exterior finishes (those finishes that can be seen and touched) are generally of greater significance than basic structural components such as wood framing and foundations.

Deterioration in the cottage interior suggested to John Eifler that all wooden structural members of the cottage's roofing system would need to be replaced with new lumber.

Many misinterpret the overall significance of historic fabric and place retention of, say, floor and roof joists as a high priority in the restoration process. Some have even gone so far as to say that Wright intended his cantilevered roofs to droop over time, thereby justifying the retention of weakened original framing members. In discussing his own buildings, Wright repeatedly referred to the significance of maintaining a horizontal roof line, i.e., crisp and straight, and the conservancy's preservation efforts were directed at replacing badly deteriorated framing to create the building Wright intended in the first place.

The philosophy adopted for the rehabilitation of the cottage was simple and straightforward: Conduct all improvements in a manner that reinforces the architect's original design intent and complements his achievements.

Most restoration projects assume that the building will be returned to a representation of a certain period in time, usually when the building was in its "heyday." Unfortunately, the cottage was never really completed during the lifetime of either the architect or client. Both Peterson and the second owners had finished the cottage with modifications which, although minor, were not in keeping with Wright's intent. John and the SPCC were forced to ask themselves a very basic and difficult question—what period would be represented when the rehabilitation was complete? The rehabilitation classification allowed for certain liberties, and after considerable deliberation it was decided to rehabilitate the cottage to a condition of "what might have been." John and the conservancy board felt that this would serve as the greatest tribute to the original owner and architect, i.e., to finally finish what they had started. This approach also allowed some modifications of Wright's design to incorporate energy conservation, handicap access, and more modern materials. The interpretive date was set at 1960, one year after the death of Wright and the year Peterson would have moved in had he lived.

Today, a large percentage of rehabilitations and restorations are carried out within the private sector by homeowners, advocacy groups, and interested corporations. In the case of the Seth Peterson Cottage, the state owned an historic and architecturally significant structure that it had left abandoned for more than 20 years. Private citizens offered to become caretakers for the site and provide a public benefit without public expense. The SPCC was able to combine the efforts of state agencies, corporations, and interested citizens to preserve a little known but significant piece of Wisconsin history.

The first hurdle in planning the project was determining the physical implications of the proposed use for the cottage. Indeed, planning for the rehabilitation was made even more difficult because no one was aware of a similar project, other than bed and breakfasts, to cite as an example to follow. Conservancy board members expressed doubts regarding the durability of the structure and the conduct of guests. Other questions arose: How many people could the cottage accommodate? Who would manage the building on a daily basis? What other functions could the cottage be used for?

The historic structure report included a number of specific recommendations regarding the physical make-up of the building and explored the feasibility of the proposed use. Ironically, the poor condition of the cottage was considered an asset in that there were no original elements such as furniture, fabrics, or custom cabinetry to be conserved as part of the work. New furnishings could easily be fabricated according to the original designs and used without concern for wear and tear.

After extensive consultation with the conservancy, John concluded in the HSR that the cottage could be used not only as a vacation rental, but also for corporate retreats and wedding receptions. John suggested that the rehabilitation incorporate the following changes from the original design to better accommodate the proposed uses:

- Incorporate a fold-out bed in the living room bench seating to provide sleeping accommodations for four.

- For corporate retreats, provide two sets of tables and seating which could be grouped for a conference setting of ten.

- Add site improvements such as a storage shed, dock, and landscaping.

Accessibility for the physically challenged was an issue that also needed to be addressed. John recommended that the cottage be converted in accordance with Americans with Disabilities Act (ADA) standards, provided that the original design was not compromised. (Wright, of course, had not considered handicap accessibility in the original design.) Accessibility was also consistent with the project mission to provide interested members of the *general public* the opportunity to experience living in a house designed by Frank Lloyd Wright. State Historical Society staff asked that the cottage be rebuilt exactly as it was, and resisted this change. They even recommended that the conservancy lobby to have the ADA standards waived. In the end, minor modifications to the rehabilitation plans (and to the original design) were all that was necessary to accommodate the physically challenged.

The State of Wisconsin is required by law to oversee the rehabilitation of a publicly owned building. The Historic Preservation Act of 1966 called for the establishment of a national practice of preserving American culture and heritage. The act required each state to establish an historic preservation office managed by a state historic preservation officer (SHPO) whose job is to establish and maintain an ongoing inventory and survey of a state's cultural resources, create and maintain a state register of historic places, make applications to the state and national registers of historic places, and encourage public education about our country's built environment. The SHPO's responsibilities also include reviewing alterations, restorations and/or demolitions of state and national register properties. The Seth Peterson Cottage was listed on both the state and national registers in the early 1980s. These designations were bestowed upon a structure that was heavily deteriorated and vandalized, but when the SPCC proposed to rehabilitate the cottage in 1989, both register listings came into regulatory play.

Register designations can be a double-edged sword. Designations are honorary titles that may create funding opportunities and lend weight to not-for-profit organizations, advocacy groups, and concerned property owners in their efforts to preserve or restore a building. However, designations may at times be a source of conflict between activists and state preservation agencies. The *Secretary of the Interior's Standards for the Rehabilitation of Historic Buildings* provides the guidelines by which SHPOs measure the retention of historic integrity. These guidelines are meant to provide a framework within which restoration or rehabilitation decisions can be made. The review process can sometimes be quite lengthy because government agencies must follow procedures that require them to scrutinize the rehabilitation proposal.

Unfortunately, the *Secretary of Interior's Standards* has developed into a document that can be interpreted in a variety of ways depending on the desired outcome. The profession appears to have reached a point where the intent of these guidelines needs to be reevaluated, as many SHPOs are using their interpretation of these guidelines as a strict set of rules rather than the loosely constructed framework that they were originally intended to be. Many preservation architects have expressed frustration over the misuse of this document. Although state agencies are meant to assist in the restoration/rehabilitation process by protecting the integrity of architectural and historic elements, they sometimes stalemate preservation by adhering to strict, no-compromise procedures.

In the case of the Seth Peterson Cottage, the State Historical Society carefully reviewed the proposed alterations/improvements to the structure. John had designed a rehabilitation that would correct much of the architectural deterioration, install Wright-designed elements that were not originally built, and add elements that were neither originally built nor originally designed—double pane windows where possible, a new shower, and handicap accessibility. John also proposed using modern materials rather than replicating the original roofing, as well as the addition of considerably more roof insulation than in the original design. State Historical Society staff felt that some of the alterations were not in keeping with the historic integrity of the "as built" cottage. A heavily contested situation resulted and a lengthy negotiation ensued. John provided technical research and documentation to support proposed alterations which the state agency eventually came to acknowledge and accept.

The Seth Peterson Cottage rehabilitation was also reviewed by the Department of Natural Resources, the Department of Administration, and the State Building Commission. State ownership, and state money that went into the cottage rehabilitation, required each of these agencies to review and approve the SPCC's proposal and design as well as each phase of rehabilitation work.

The conservancy learned that rehabilitating a state property opened up a Pandora's box of issues and concerns which many private property owners do not encounter. Many private rehabilitations fall under the jurisdiction of a local landmarks commission which enforces a municipal landmarks ordinance. Often, if a privately owned structure has been landmarked or included within an historic district, the landmarks commission conducts the review of alterations, additions, or demolitions to that property or district. A local landmarks commission is often required to make a decision within a set time frame, thereby ensuring the owner of due process. Because several state agencies were involved with the cottage rehabilitation, the SPCC had to adapt to their review policies and procedures. Receiving the necessary approvals took months at a time. The SPCC's proposals had to be well prepared and documented prior to meetings with the DNR/DOA/SHS. Multiple design schemes and drawings were prepared for each agency review. Often the agencies would concur with partial acceptance of some concepts and suggest further refinement of others.

More often than not, state agencies operate independently. It was clear from the start that each agency associated with the project had its own agenda. Kermit Traska, Southern District Supervisor for Wisconsin State Parks, provided the professional coordination needed to properly navigate the project through the approval process. As the project manager for the DNR, Kermit provided invaluable assis-

Kermit Traska helped the conservancy deal with the state agencies.

tance and advice to the conservancy as well as coordination of the various state agencies to keep the project moving along. He helped draft the 15-year lease that gave the conservancy the right to rehabilitate and operate the cottage. In November 1989 Kermit drafted a general responsibilities document which identified individuals and agencies and explained their role in the Seth Peterson Cottage rehabilitation process:

"Kermit Traska shall act as the coordinator for comments from the Architect/SPCC to the agencies and from the agencies to the Architect/SPCC. This is to ensure clear communications and to make sure that those individuals who need to know are informed. The Architect working with the SPCC submits preliminary plans for the design phase to the DNR for review and comment by DNR, DOA and SHS. The DNR will coordinate meetings between the Architect/SPCC and the agencies to come to agreement on issues that remain unresolved. Each individual or agency has an important role to play in the project. It is vitally important that everyone work together to come up with the best product for the long-term care of the cottage."

Kermit also recognized that DNR rules prohibiting overnight lodging in state park buildings would have to be changed. He worked with department staff to effect that change as negotiations with SHS and DOA continued. Other DNR staff were responsible for cottage-related activities at Mirror Lake State Park, for DNR review of the rehabilitation plans, and for processing a state grant to the conservancy. Department of Administration staff were to approve the rehabilitation plans and ensure that the State Building Commission (a commission composed of the governor, legislators, and citizens that must approve major construction projects on state properties) received information and acted when necessary. The State Historical Society staff reviewed rehabilitation plans to ensure that state and federal historic preservation laws and guidelines were followed.

The general responsibilities document was beneficial because it outlined how the agencies were to interact with one another and explained that the goal of organizing the project was expediency and cooperation between the agencies and the SPCC: "Each person or agency has a stake in the rehabilitation of the cottage with the ultimate goal of long-term use and maintenance of the facility. Some interests are based on statutory obligations and some may be based on personal interests."

Kermit also helped John and the conservancy comply with regulations of other state agencies. These included meeting state building codes, meeting state codes regulating provision of overnight accommodations, and meeting ADA requirements.

John, who was well versed in dealing with state agencies, represented the conservancy in meeting most requirements. To ensure that everyone was clear about their agreements, John recorded minutes of all meetings held with the agencies. The minutes held each party accountable for their actions. Without a continuing effort to communicate with each agency, the conservancy's proposal and subsequent rehabilitation work might never have been approved.

Even with Kermit acting as guide through the maze of state bureaucracy, the project repeatedly encountered design review concerns from the agencies, most notably the SHS and the DOA. Some agency staff felt that they had a responsibility to retain the historic integrity of the cottage as built. They intended to preserve the quirks of the built structure, even if those quirks were not designed by Wright. They did not feel that the as-designed perspective presented by the architect should be incorporated in the rehabilitation if those systems were never actually used, and they were opposed to adding the proposed new elements that were not in the original design, elements that John and the conservancy felt were necessary to make the cottage successful as a vacation rental. Back and forth went Eifler, the SPCC, and the agencies with redesigned plans and redrawn concepts, tying up both time and money. Each set of new architectural drawings cost the SPCC money that would have been better used on the rehabilitation. At one point construction was stalled until a compromise agreement on the heating system was reached. The agreement called for leaving in the original forced air system and adding the in-floor radiant heating as intended by Wright. At another point, the conservancy asked a state legislator to intervene with the agencies to reach an agreement on an issue related to new windows. Although the state officers felt they were doing their jobs as required by law, the SPCC bore the expense of the decision-making process, spending valuable capital which had been acquired by fundraising.

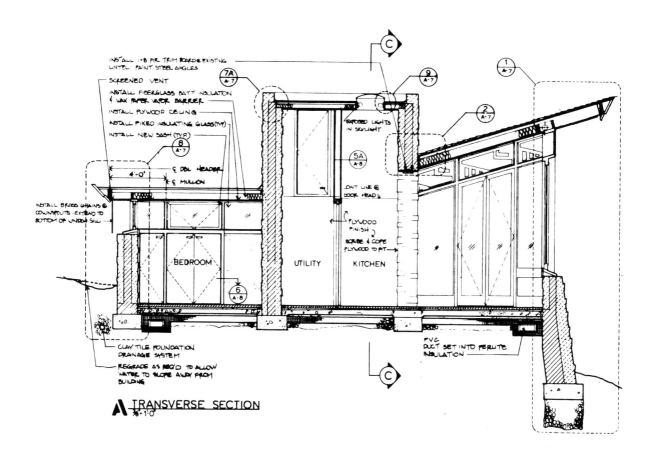

INSTALL 1×8 FIR TRIM BOARD @ EXISTING
LINTEL. PAINT STEEL ANGLES

SCREENED VENT

INSTALL FIBERGLASS BATT INSULATION
& WAX PAPER VAPOR BARRIER

INSTALL PLYWOOD CEILING

INSTALL FIXED INSULATING GLASS (TYP)

INSTALL NEW SASH (TYP)

⌀ DBL HEADER

⌀ MULLION

4'-0"

INSTALL BRASS CHAINS @
DOWNSPOUTS · EXTEND TO
BOTTOM OF WINDOW SILL

EXPOSED LIGHTS
IN SKYLIGHT

JOINT LINE @
DOOR HEAD

PLYWOOD
FINISH

SCRIBE & COPE
PLYWOOD TO FIT

BEDROOM   UTILITY   KITCHEN

CLAY TILE FOUNDATION
DRAINAGE SYSTEM

REGRADE AS REQ'D TO ALLOW
WATER TO SLOPE AWAY FROM
BUILDING

PVC
DUCT SET INTO PERLITE
INSULATION

TRANSVERSE SECTION
⅜" · 1'-0"

Construction drawing for the rehabilitation prepared by Eifler & Associates.

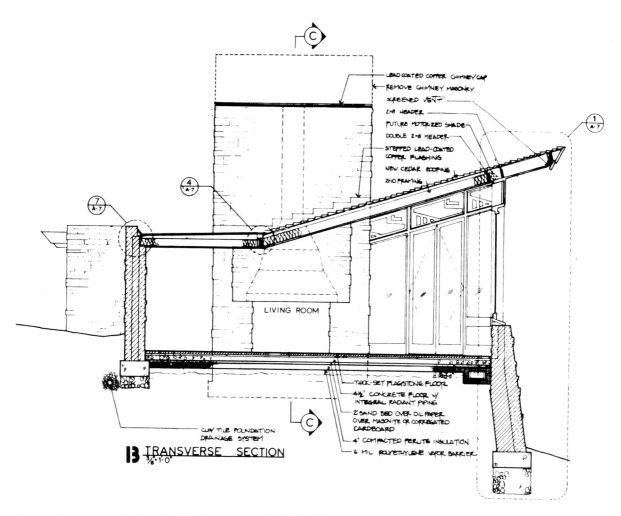

LEAD COATED COPPER CHIMNEY CAP
REMOVE CHIMNEY MASONRY
SCREENED VENT
2×8 HEADER
FUTURE MOTORIZED SHADE
DOUBLE 2×8 HEADER
STEPPED LEAD-COATED COPPER FLASHING
NEW CEDAR ROOFING
2×10 FRAMING

LIVING ROOM

THICK-SET FLAGSTONE FLOOR
4½" CONCRETE FLOOR W/ INTEGRAL RADIANT PIPING
2" SAND BED OVER OIL PAPER OVER MASONITE OR CORREGATED CARDBOARD
4" COMPACTED PERLITE INSULATION
6 MIL POLYETHYLENE VAPOR BARRIER

CLAY TILE FOUNDATION DRAINAGE SYSTEM

13 TRANSVERSE SECTION
⅛"·1'-0"

Construction drawing for the rehabilitation prepared by Eifler & Associates.

Perhaps the greatest lesson learned by all parties involved in the public-private partnership was that the relationship often became a test of compromise. Each negotiating party (architect, state agencies, SPCC) made sacrifices to further rehabilitation progress. For example, John developed the design components with a series of options rather than a single solution to solicit feedback and comments from each participant. Compromise was reached by constant communication of objectives, supported with documented testing and research to justify the methods used. Two keys for a successful rehabilitation undertaking such as the Seth Peterson Cottage are constant communication between all parties involved and the patience to work with and learn from each party to reach a common goal.

In addition to learning how to "network" within the complex realm of state government agencies, the conservancy received an education about how to manage a rehabilitation project. From humble beginnings as an amateur, uncoordinated, and naive group, a group of committed citizens transformed themselves into an efficient, knowledgeable, and professional not-for-profit organization.

In 1989, as the group incorporated as the Seth Peterson Cottage Conservancy, a project management plan began to form. Board members started to view the rehabilitation as a series of segments, or points along a path which would eventually connect. The board of directors divided into committees for fundraising, construction, public relations/events, merchandising, accounting, and legal work. Operating as independent functions under the umbrella of the board, committee members could concentrate on specific goals. Frequent board meetings (bi-weekly at first, then monthly) were scheduled so that ideas and progress could be shared and plans changed as necessary.

The conservancy first had to evaluate the scope of the project before beginning a capital campaign, and develop estimates of the financial benefits of the project. Essentially, how much money was needed to produce the finished product, and what revenue would be generated upon its completion?

Preservation is not and should not be driven by economics. Frank Lloyd Wright said, "A culture based solely on Commerce is no culture at all." The cottage was not rehabilitated for financial reasons. The Mirror Lake residents, and preservationists from throughout the Midwest, recognized the small building as having cultural value. They appreciated Wright's artistic expression of nature inherent within the cottage's design and materials. Furthermore, the SPCC respected Seth Peterson's personal struggle to produce his own mark upon the community. What is important in this case is how the SPCC went about financing the rehabilitation and the goals they set for the completed cottage.

As part of the preliminary study for the cottage rehabilitation, John and the conservancy analyzed the estimated costs and the likely financial benefits of the proposed rental use. This simple cost-benefit analysis early in the project planning stages predicted that an occupancy rate of only 36% was required for the project to "break even" on day-to-day cottage operations. Any funds generated from a higher occupancy rate could be used to create an endowment to offset future maintenance and repair expenses. An analysis of this type is a key part of the planning for historic restoration. If an organization can predict a modicum of profitability, the prospects of a successful project are greatly improved.

The SPCC had to prepare a solid estimate of the funding required to rehabilitate the cottage from a deteriorated shell back into an architecturally significant design that could stand up to constant visitor use. John estimated that the rehabilitation would cost $250,000. With an understanding of the financial scope of the project, the SPCC was able to plan an aggressive capital campaign. It is extremely rare to find a preservation project that can be planned and constructed non-stop from start to finish. It takes time to thoroughly plan the project, gain consensus, gather support, and most importantly, raise money to pay for and administer the work.

The cottage was seriously deteriorated. John felt that some problems should be tackled immediately, fearing that there would otherwise be little left to preserve. In an effort to protect the remaining original material and allow for progress through the fundraising period, the construction work was divided into three phases:

Phase I. Deconstruction and Roof Construction: This involved the removal and cataloging of all original material to be retained for the project. Construction of the new roof would protect remaining masonry and demonstrate progress on the preservation effort for ongoing fundraising.

Phase II. Remaining Cottage Construction: This included completion of the exterior and interior walls, mechanical, electrical, plumbing, and interior cabinetry and trim.

Phase III. Cottage Furnishing and Site Work: The final phase included completion of the interior furnishings such as furniture, fabrics, and appliances. The dock, landscaping, and storage building are also included in this phase.

The optimistic and inexperienced conservancy board had originally expected to complete the entire rehabilitation project in about 18 months. The schedule allowed six months for organizing and planning, followed by a year of simultaneously raising money and doing the actual rehabilitation. They hoped to open the cottage to visitors in September 1990. Not surprisingly, they had seriously underestimated the time needed to negotiate with state agencies, raise money, find contractors, and do the work. As it turned out, Phase I was completed during the period from spring of 1990 through the winter of 1991. Then the conservancy ran out of money. Phase II was delayed as fundraising continued. Finally, in spring of 1992 enough money had been raised and work resumed. The third phase was completed in 1995 with construction of the dock. Thus, the main project work took nearly three years, and follow-up work, such as the dock and landscaping, took even longer. The cottage was dedicated in June 1992.

The rehabilitation was divided into phases primarily so that the SPCC could manage their debt. Construction proceeded according to what could be done with available funds, sometimes referred to as "fundable bundles." Construction bids were solicited for each phase and matched with fundraising. This approach allowed the SPCC to prepare for capital expenses without building piles of debt, although, as noted above, it did draw out the construction work.

FUNDRAISING

The Seth Peterson Cottage eventually cost $350,000 to rehabilitate. (The increase over the original $250,000 estimate was due to the costs of furnishing and equipping the cottage, building the storage shed and the dock, completing the landscaping, and other extras that were not in John's original analysis.) When the conservancy started fundraising, members had virtually no experience and no contact with foundations and other funding sources. They soon discovered that money should be the primary concern of any group undertaking a rehabilitation project, whether large or small, and a capital campaign must be carefully planned before any rehabilitation work begins. More often than not, design and construction expenses run over budget, leaving many groups with a project that is difficult to complete. Yet the process of raising capital is neither a cut-and-dried nor easily understood task. Fundraising is a humbling experience because a fundraising group must aggressively seek funds from both familiar and unfamiliar sources and must continue until the project is finished and debt is eliminated. The cottage rehabilitation is an enlightening example of how one group of committed citizens pursued a capital campaign that was to prove difficult, frustrating (although educational), and ultimately successful.

In 1989, the SPCC established a fundraising goal of $250,000 to cover all three phases of rehabilitation. State officials were approached only after the SPCC understood the amount of money needed to fulfill their vision for the cottage.

At first, the idea of a private not-for-profit organization asking the state for funding to rehabilitate a state-owned property appeared to be a losing proposition. The state had allocated only a minimum of funding toward the cottage, mainly to keep out vandals. However, Audrey Laatsch, president of the SPCC, believed the DNR had a responsibility to contribute to the preservation of this historically significant property. Sandra Shaw, fundraiser for the State Historical Society, provided important advice to SPCC: "You have to determine the future use [of the project] before you can raise any funds. You can't ask someone for money if you can't tell them what you'll be doing with the building once it's finished. Matching funds or grants from the state or federal government should be applied for. No one likes to be the first to give, but everyone is willing to join the crowd. Also, by showing that the state is interested, it is easier to get private individuals to donate."

On the advice of SHS staff, Audrey contacted State Representative Dale Schultz of Sauk County, who became an advocate for the cottage. He drafted an amendment to the 1989-91 state budget legislation which allocated $50,000 from the state for a matching funds grant for the cottage. The proposed grant would provide $25,000 in seed money for rehabilitation with the condition that the SPCC raise a matching $50,000 in order to receive the second $25,000 installment. With the help of various individuals, including State Representative Margaret Lewis and Jeff Neubauer, then chair of the State Democratic Party, the conservancy was able to secure a favorable legislative vote and ensure that Governor Tommy Thompson would support the grant. Representative Lewis played a pivotal role in explaining to the governor the viability of the conservancy's proposal and the significance of a long-forgotten Wright structure. Soon after the governor signed the budget, the SPCC received the initial $25,000 to begin the long-awaited cottage rehabilitation. Conservancy leaders thus learned early on that having political support for a project can be extremely helpful.

The conservancy also applied for 501(c)(3) status with state and federal governments. This tax filing status exempts a not-for-profit organization from taxes on all income derived through fundraising and asset acquisition. As a 501(c)(3) organization, the SPCC could embark on an aggressive fundraising campaign and membership drive. A major fundraising drive to match the $50,000 state grant ensued, and in-kind donations, the value of which counted toward the matching grant, were solicited to significantly lower labor and material expenses.

With the state matching grant and 501(c)(3) status approved, the SPCC Board of Directors developed a long-range fundraising plan. By March 1990 the SPCC had developed a brochure which provided potential donors with a mission statement describing the rehabilitation proposal and how contributions would be used. Also included in the brochure was a schedule of donor categories ranging from a $15 individual membership to a $1,000 patron.

The conservancy also began a member newsletter and offered premiums ranging from color photos of the cottage to rental discounts for major donors. Most conservancy membership funds were used for the daily operating expenses (printing, postage, etc.) while larger donations went toward rehabilitation expenses. The conservancy targeted solicitations from donors who were interested in experiencing a Frank Lloyd Wright environment firsthand and who would appreciate the uniqueness of the cottage design. The conservancy also made money—and publicized the project—by selling T-shirts, framed architect's renderings of the cottage, and notecards with a drawing of the cottage. Additional donations were received as a result of publicity about the cottage in newspapers and magazines. Board member Bill Martinelli graphically reproduced the cottage's flagstone floor design originally used as a map to remove and reconstruct the floor. This map provided the means by which individual donors could "sponsor" a stone for a $200 donation.

Although the first conservancy board of directors lacked a basic standard of fundraising, i.e., connections with philanthropic individuals and organizations, they quickly learned that the board needed to be enlarged to include members with specific professional skills and contacts. They realized that a diverse board comprised of members who could approach personal acquaintances for contributions, whether in funding, services, or in-kind donations, was a key to success. In general, relying on personal connections for help may seem awkward, but often those relationships represent the largest component of a fund-raising effort.

John and conservancy board members were able to secure donations of both money and building materials through their personal and professional contacts. For example, board member Mary Lawson, a partner in a Madison architecture firm, used her contacts with suppliers and contractors in the building trades and secured a Burnham Boiler from General Heating Contractors, a Madison supplier with whom Lawson had worked previously. The board kept detailed accounts of monetary and in-kind

Pella Windows donated custom windows and double-pane glass for the large front wall, rear ribbon windows, and storage shed.

Photograph by Beth Singer, courtesy Pella Windows

Wright's use of proportion and scale produce a large open room, connecting nature and structure.
Photograph by Beth Singer, courtesy Pella Windows

The finished living room settle, chairs, and table.
Photograph by Eric Wallner

The bedroom and bathroom are removed from the large open living space and tucked behind the massive hearth. The bedroom is connected to the larger room by a short, almost nonexistent, corridor. No doors impede the spatial flow.
Photograph by Eric Wallner

The Seth Peterson Cottage "contains more architecture per square foot than any building Wright ever built."

Photograph by Toni Soluri. Courtesy Architectural Digest. © 1993 The Conde Nast Publications. Used with permission.

The battered stone terrace walls and soaring roof give the cottage a monumentality that belies its small size.
Photograph by Beth Singer, courtesy Pella Windows

With its fireplace and in-floor heating, the cottage is popular year-round.
Photograph by Lois Majerus

At night the roof appears to float over the living space.
Photograph by Beth Singer, courtesy Pella Windows

John Eifler created this rendering of the cottage which became the image most associated with the rehabilitation. The SPCC uses the image as part of a nationally distributed fundraising/merchandising program which includes T-shirts, notecards, framed prints, and jewelry.

donations so contributions could be accurately applied toward matching grants. Without the work of the board members enlisting contacts to make in-kind donations, the SPCC would have been hard pressed to meet their matching grant targets. In-kind contributions eventually totaled roughly $100,000, nearly a third of the total cost of the rehabilitation.

By providing in-kind contributions to the conservancy, corporate sponsors and product manufacturers received two benefits. First, they could deduct the cost of manufacturing the product from their net year-end taxable income. Second, products contributed to the rehabilitation provided the manufacturers with name recognition through the association with Frank Lloyd Wright and preservation. For example, Pella Windows used pictures of the cottage with their windows in national building trade journal advertisements. Many of the product contributors were Wisconsin-based manufacturers who felt a sense of responsibility toward a Wisconsin Frank Lloyd Wright structure and a Wisconsin not-for-profit organization. This was not a unique situation, as many not-for-profits should and do solicit regional businesses for support. Yet with the Seth Peterson Cottage rehabilitation the amount of local support was staggering and very much appreciated.

In early 1990 the SPCC board concluded that they did not have sufficient expertise, experience, or time to pursue fundraising on their own. In an attempt to devise a more structured and organized method of seeking funds, they enlisted the help of a small Milwaukee-based fundraising consulting firm willing to take on the effort of raising a "mere" $250,000. The consultant identified 75 potential grant foundation sources. From a solicitation mailing to the 75 foundations, the SPCC received only three contributions totaling $5,000. The consultant also arranged a fundraising function with a tour of Frank Lloyd Wright's 1908 Gilmore House and the 1936 Jacobs I House, both in Madison, which raised $2,050. The consultants also initially contacted Ver Halen, Inc., a Wisconsin-based window distributor, which helped to secure the custom Pella windows for the cottage and the newly designed storage shed.

The consultant, however, was not well versed in construction and rehabilitation projects. After spending approximately $12,000 for the consultant's services, board members realized that the cost was not justified in terms of the grants received and discontinued the consultant's services. Nevertheless, the consultant taught the SPCC that fundraising needed to be accomplished by the organization itself; the consultant could only identify possible sources. The conservancy continued to seek out grant and foundation sources throughout the remainder of the rehabilitation and well into 1992, sending out 85 letters of request to U.S. foundations and another 33 to Japanese foundations.

To generate further contributions, the SPCC hosted several fundraising events, including a cocktail party, tour, and dinner at the Frank Lloyd Wright-designed Bogk House in Milwaukee, a silent auction brunch in Madison, and an evening with Frank Lloyd Wright's grandson, Eric Lloyd Wright. A fundraising event in November 1991 at Wisconsin Dells Greyhound Race Track netted $12,000. Reflecting on the fundraising events, Audrey Laatsch stated that "fundraising events are hard work, and usually brought in less money than anticipated. However, these events were great for publicity and spread the word to potential donors."

State Historical Society staff were able to direct two

Audrey Laatsch.

Tom Garver led the conservancy's fundraising.

matching grants totaling $17,000 to the conservancy. The grants allowed SPCC to apply in-kind donations of services and materials toward those grants. In October 1990, the SPCC was awarded its only non-matching grant of $10,000 from the Andy Warhol Foundation of New York City. At times when fundraising lagged, Audrey Laatsch made personal loans to the conservancy to cover expenses. Barbara Elsner, an advisor to the conservancy and owner of a Wright house, also provided two loans of $7,500 each through the George L. N. Meyer Family Foundation.

Board member Tom Garver coordinated most of the fundraising efforts and prepared a detailed explanation of the project which was used to solicit foundation grants. In October 1991, as a result of Tom's efforts the Jeffris Family Foundation of Janesville, Wisconsin, awarded the conservancy an $80,000 matching grant. The Jeffris Family Foundation supports preservation of historic buildings in rural and small Wisconsin communities. The Jeffris grant gave the SPCC a much needed "second wind" to complete the rehabilitation. The grant allowed the conservancy to match the $80,000 with in-kind donations of services and materials. Applicable contributions had to be new donations that were not already pledged as of October 1991.

In December 1991 the board decided to dedicate the cottage on June 7, 1992. Both Seth Peterson and Frank Lloyd Wright were born on June 8, and June 8, 1992, was the 125th anniversary of Wright's birth. In December 1991, however, the reconstruction of the stone slab floor and radiant heating, electrical, plumbing, and installation of the new windows had yet to be completed. Materials and services had already been donated, but were waiting to be installed. With a deadline looming, work was accelerated, and all the major work on the cottage was completed by early June.

By May 1992 the SPCC had raised half the Jeffris Family Foundation matching grant funds. With the June 1 Jeffris grant deadline fast approaching, the SPCC shifted into high gear. Foundation president Tom Jeffris agreed to extend the deadline to June 10 so the contributions received at the cottage dedication could count toward the grant match. Between May 24 and June 10 the SPCC raised the last

Tom Jeffris, president of the Jeffris Family Foundation, largest contributor to the rehabilitation.

$35,000 needed to match the Jeffris Family Foundation grant. By June 7, 1992, the SPCC had raised over $250,000 in grants, in-kind donations, and pledges. (The pledges had to be paid by September 1992 to count toward the Jeffris grant. Virtually all were.)

After the dedication, the conservancy still owed $27,000 to contractors for various construction services. The conservancy continued fundraising to pay off the remaining construction debt and to pay for completion of the new storage shed John had designed. All outstanding debts, including the loans from Audrey Laatsch and the George L. N. Meyer Family Foundation, were paid off by June 1995.

PART 3

THE REHABILITATION

■ ■ ■

The cottage had to be "deconstructed" as the first step in rehabilitation.

■ PART 3 • THE REHABILITATION

The first rehabilitation work began in fall of 1989 when John Eifler, Audrey Laatsch, and a group of volunteers removed the boards from the cottage windows and began to search for materials that could be salvaged. Aside from assessing the state of the cottage and removing some of the wood trim for later use, volunteers could do little because the building was so seriously deteriorated that hard hats and special equipment were needed. Fortunately, the conservancy was able to obtain the services of the Wisconsin Conservation Corps (WCC), a state program that provides training and work experience for young people. Two six-person WCC crews spent four weeks each at the cottage during April and May 1990 doing the Phase I deconstruction.

The term "deconstruction" is sometimes used instead of "demolition" because it better defines the process of removing material from a building that is undergoing preservation work. A separate set of drawings showed the WCC crews which items were to be removed and what was to be done with them. Three categories of building components were defined. The first category

Volunteers removed the boards from the cottage windows.

Bill Martinelli (l), John Eifler (c), and a volunteer examine cottage drawings.

was material to be removed and discarded. This included the roof framing and plywood ceiling finishes. Samples were saved for duplication. The second category included building components such as kitchen cabinets, operable sash, and light fixtures which were removed and set aside for measuring and replicating. Finally, components to be reused in the project, such as the plywood clerestory panels and the stone flooring, were carefully numbered and stored either on site or in a nearby barn.

The WCC crews removed the roof and all the remaining woodwork, the flagstone floor, and the concrete pad under the flagstones. Finally, they removed all the heating ducts and the old electrical system. The crews cut down a number of trees in the new cottage parking area at the head of the driveway. They also removed some trees on the hillside below the cottage to open up the view to Mirror Lake. They sliced the larger tree trunks into foot-thick chunks and used them as steps on a newly created path to the lakeshore.

When the crews were finished, only the sandstone walls and fireplace remained. The cottage was ready to be put back together.

ROOF

Wright always attached significance to the type of roof chosen for his houses. As the cottage was a small commission, Wright probably tried to keep costs down by using forms that had proven less costly in the past. In *The Natural House* he states:

"Now the shape of roof—whether a shed roof, a hip roof or a flat roof—depends in part on expediency and in part on your personal taste or knowledge as to what is appropriate in the circumstances. One of the advantages of the sloping roof is that it gives you a sense of spaciousness inside, a sense of overhead uplift which I often feel to be very good. The flat roof also has advantages in construction. It is easy to do, of course. . . . The cheapest roof, however, is the shed roof—the roof sloping one way, more or less. There you get more for your money than you can get from any other form of roof. . . But the type of roof you choose must not only deal with the elements in your region but be appropriate to the circumstances, according to your personal preference. . . ."

Though the cottage has been described as a "building all under one roof," the roof is, in fact, very complex. It is comprised of a large sloping shed roof and two levels of flat roof, an upper one above the kitchen and bathroom/storage loft, and another over the bedroom and the rear of the living room. The flat roof over the kitchen has parapet walls, while the roof over the living room and bedroom has large overhangs in some areas and parapet walls in others.

WCC crew removing the bedroom roof.

John found that the original roof joists were installed contrary to the original drawings; instead of every third joist resting on vertical supports, none did. The joists appeared to be supported by the decorative plywood clerestory panels located between the vertical supports. These panels are made of a sheet of double-strength glass sandwiched between two layers of 3/4-inch plywood. Some architectural historians have likened Wright's use of cut-out ornamental patterns in his Usonian homes to the intricate art glass designs used in his early Prairie houses decades before. There is a marked difference between the two, in that the ornamental panels

The cottage was deconstructed and the deteriorated roofs removed, leaving the salvaged vertical supports and the original masonry construction.

designed by Wright for the Seth Peterson Cottage are structural and serve to transfer the load of the roof joists over to the vertical supports. Wright, in *The Natural House*, refers to these panels as "integral ornament" or "the nature pattern of actual construction." Though the practice is risky (the glass in two of the panels was cracked, presumably due to the weight of the roof), it simplified the original framing, as no header is required to support the joists between the vertical supports. No one was comfortable with the prospect of essentially leaving glass as a supporting element, and John proposed installing new joists with conventional flush headers over the clerestory panels to transfer the load of the roof directly to the vertical supports.

The roof was designed to allow water to flow off the living room shed roof and onto the flat roof segment that extends over the bedroom and the rear of the living room. John found that the flat roof was installed perfectly level, and over time the structure had deflected, creating depressions in which water pooled, and which eventually leaked. This lack of proper drainage was inconsistent with Wright's intentions:

"But with the flat roof you must devise ways and means of getting rid of the water. One way to do this is to build, on top of the flat, a slight pitch to the eaves. This may be done by 'furring.' There are various ways of getting water off a flat roof. But it must be done." (*The Natural House*)

The rehabilitation plan called for two improvements to correct this problem. First, a scupper was added at the living room parapet wall to provide a direct path for water to flow off the roof. Second, the plywood sheathing for the flat roof areas was placed on a series of tapered furring strips attached directly to the flat roof framing to ensure a very slight pitch as Wright recommended. Water drains from the bedroom flat roof through three copper-pipe roof drains that allow the water to fall clear of the exterior wall. Bronze drip chains were added to reduce splashing when the water hits the ground and to encourage the formation of icicles.

The plywood clerestory panels had been protected by the wide overhanging eaves of the sloped roof.

The shed roof over the living room was originally specified as cedar shingles nailed to 1 x 8 sheathing. Typically cedar shingles are applied to roofs no flatter than a 4 in 12 (rise to run) roof slope. Wright, ever the optimist, designed the roof slope to be 3-1/2 to 12. During the rehabilitation a special

Audrey Laatsch and Tom Ryan with newly completed roof framing.

roofing sub-base known as Ice and Water Shield was installed beneath the cedar shingles to help guard against leaks and ice dams. The flat segments of the roof were originally sealed with a conventional 4-ply asphalt roof which is durable but requires considerable maintenance and has a relatively short life span. After considerable discussion with State Historical Society staff, who wanted to use asphalt roofing as was done originally, EPDM roofing was installed. EPDM is a relatively new roofing material comprised of a single sheet of "synthetic neoprene" that has proven to have superior performance and durability for buildings with minimal slope roofs, providing the sheathing's underside is properly vented externally.

Originally, the roof structure contained only two inches of insulation, causing heavy snow to melt quickly from heat loss. John recommended that the maximum amount of insulation be installed as part of the rehabilitation work. Preservation, by its very nature, should work hand-in-hand with energy conservation and every effort should be made to reduce energy consumption. One of the best methods of ensuring preservation of an historic building is to keep the monthly utility costs as low as possible. The

By late 1990, the new roof members were in place. When the roof was completed, a lead-coated copper cricket was added to protect the sandstone masonry and aid in water discharge.

By spring 1991, the newly constructed shed roof and rear flat roofs were complete.

The narrow vertical supports complement the wide expanse of yet-to-be-installed glass, enhancing the "floating" sensation of the shed roof.

cavity between the 2 x 10 framing was filled with eight inches of batt insulation. The remaining two inches were left open for air circulation to help prevent moisture buildup. Screened air vents were carefully installed at the perimeter of the roof to ensure sufficient air flow.

MASONRY

The buff sandstone for the masonry walls, chimney, and flooring of the cottage was quarried in nearby Rock Springs and had stood up well through the years. Although sandstone is usually considered a soft stone, the local type has proven to be very durable. The stone was originally designed to be laid up as a masonry wall with a layer of board insulation separating the two faces, but for some unexplained

The durable mass of sandstone masonry was quarried from a local deposit. The chimney was integrated into the overall masonry mass surrounding the kitchen and bath. Owen Pritchard added seven feet of masonry atop the chimney.

reason the insulation was eliminated and replaced by an inner wythe of concrete block. This construction alteration had a significant impact on comfort, as the exterior masonry walls of the cottage were virtually uninsulated. Aside from mild cleaning inside and out, the stone walls were left intact. The cottage has only recently required selective tuckpointing maintenance.

The fireplace and chimney were problematic from the start. As designed by Wright, the chimney was integrated into the overall masonry mass surrounding the kitchen and bath. The terminus of the chimney was undifferentiated and was the same height as the adjacent masonry walls. At first, everyone wondered why the second owners had added a seven-foot-tall extension to the chimney. In the fall of 1989 the mystery was solved. On a cool clear Saturday, a group of volunteers descended on the cottage to remove the protective plywood panels and clean up the site. They decided it would be fun to start a

Pritchard's addition to the chimney was reduced as much as possible given current building codes. Note the cricket where the roof meets the masonry, lower right.

fire in the fireplace as a symbolic gesture of the cottage reawakening. Within minutes after lighting the fire, the volunteers stumbled out of the cottage coughing and rubbing their eyes. Smoke billowed out of the doors and windows. The fire was pouring smoke back into the room despite the fact that the damper was fully open. It was obvious that the second owner had added the height to the chimney in an effort to eliminate a backdraft problem, obviously to no avail.

A local chimney company called Top Hat analyzed the problem and concluded that the chimney extension did little to rectify the problem and could therefore be removed. Top Hat also recommended that the large rectangular flue be converted to a circular shape, as smoke has a tendency to spiral its way up the chimney, and a circular flue, though smaller in area, would produce a smoother and more effective draw. A new damper was added atop the chimney and the original damper left open to keep the flue

The cut sandstone walls have a texture that was typical of Wright in the 1950s. The indentations above the kitchen entry indicate the placement of roof joists.

An air duct was installed under the foundation and up through the floor to the fireplace.

warm, which would also increase chimney draw when a fire was first started. Finally, a pipe was run beneath the floor and outer wall to a remote exterior intake vent to supply fresh air at the front of the fire. These changes improved the fireplace draw immensely. Unfortunately, even with these changes the height of the chimney could be reduced to only 18 inches above the adjacent masonry due to building code and fire safety restrictions.

DOORS AND WINDOWS

One of Frank Lloyd Wright's special talents was to use the relative proportions of building components for drama and effect. Much has been written about the use of contrasting ceiling heights to create dramatic entrances and give the effect of large open rooms. But his genius lies in the thoroughness with which he used proportion and scale to achieve these effects. In the case of the cottage, the relative-

The sloping roof, supported by an extremely light wall of glass, makes the cottage seem larger than its 880 square feet.

ly small building is made to feel larger by the use of a dramatically sloped roof supported by an extremely light, almost fragile wall of glass. The building also appears larger because of Wright's insistence on wooden supports that were designed to be as narrow as possible. In typical wood frame construction, the vertical supports or studs are installed at regular intervals. Window frames and sash are placed between the supports. The space between the window frame and the stud is usually covered with a length of window trim, or casing, about four inches wide. When one considers that the window sash is an additional two inches wide, a conventional window wall would be regularly interrupted by sash and trim in excess of eight inches. In the Seth Peterson Cottage, the casement window sash is attached directly to the stud and the adjacent fixed glass is held in place with a narrow 3/4-inch glazing stop. In this manner, Wright reduces the amount of trim required and creates a delicate window wall interrupted by sash and vertical supports that are only four inches wide. This sophisticated support and glazing system creates an effect of larger windows due to the narrow relative size of the supporting elements and creates a roof that seems to float over the enclosed space below.

Wright had specified solid brass piano hinges for all the cottage doors and windows, but standard three-inch steel hinges were used instead, probably to save money. The piano hinges would have provided an additional strengthening element to the door and window frames.

When inspecting the condition of the original windows and terrace doors, John surmised that they had probably been fabricated on site with a table saw. The joinery had separated due to abuse and the shrinking of the soft yellow pine. A number of glass panels were either cracked or broken. Although Wright had designed screens, it was clear that the screens originally installed on the cottage were not designed in accordance with the original drawings. As mentioned previously, the decorative clerestory panels protected by the roof overhang were found to be in good condition and were ultimately incorporated into the preserved cottage.

Before any work was planned for the cottage, John completed an energy study to assess the overall insulation abilities of the building shell. Built during a period of cheap energy, everyone assumed the cottage would require some remedial energy conservation measures to reduce maintenance costs. John was surprised when the energy study showed that the structure would be virtually impossible to heat during the coldest winter days. The low insulation value of the masonry walls, combined with large areas of single-pane glass, resulted in a building that on the coldest days would be difficult to maintain at a temperature of 50 degrees—obviously unsuitable for a winter vacation rental.

Because the rehabilitation philosophy was one of conservation as well as improvement, John recommended that the cottage insulation be upgraded not only by adding roof insulation but also by installing new window sash that incorporated double-pane glass where possible. The clerestory panels and mitred corner windows would remain single-pane. Department of Administration and State Historical Society staff vehemently opposed the substitution of double-pane glass for single-pane glass. The original design called for single-pane windows, but in this case, as with the flat roof, John pointed out that more modern materials would conserve energy, last much longer, and not detract from the aesthetics of the building. Using double-pane glass would allow the cottage to be rented year round. John also pointed out that condensation that forms on the inside face of single-pane glass in winter would cause water damage to the wooden sill below; double-pane glass would virtually eliminate this problem. The Department of Administration and the State Historical Society would not budge, concerned with what

Pella workmen installing the custom windows. This photo shows the narrow vertical supports beneath the shed roof.

they called "precedence," though double-pane glass has been approved in many rehabilitation projects throughout the country. The conservancy requested that the proposal be reviewed by a higher authority, in this case the National Park Service.

The case was forwarded to a National Park Service review official by the State Historical Society. John called the Park Service and discovered that a substantial portion of the information, notably the energy study, was not included in the packet forwarded by the state. John sent the missing information directly to the National Park Service and eventually the double-pane glass was approved. This episode was a reminder that it is important to make direct contact with any key third parties that are involved in discussions about the project.

Pella Windows was contacted through the local supplier, Ver Halen, and asked to help out on the project. Realizing the significance of the project, Pella generously donated custom-fabricated replacement windows that duplicate the originals. Ver Halen provided a team of carpenters, who arrived wearing matching blue jumpsuits, to install the windows. This time the window sash was attached to the frame with brass piano hinges, consistent with the original design. The mitred-glass corner windows were left as single-pane units, as at that time no one made that type of window from double-pane glass. Pella now manufactures a mitred-glass double-pane corner window unit, and conservancy board members like to think that it was the cottage that provided the inspiration for this product.

The single-pane, mitred-glass corners are characteristic of Wright's work.

MECHANICAL, ELECTRICAL, AND PLUMBING

The cottage was originally designed to be heated with a radiant floor system like the one Wright first used in the 1936 Jacobs I House. When the cottage was built, a conventional forced-air system was substituted, probably to reduce costs. In considering various heating alternatives for the rehabilitation, the energy study concluded it would be nearly impossible to provide adequate comfort with a forced-air

system. As it was the intent of the rehabilitation to finish the cottage in accord with Wright's design, John recommended that a contemporary version of the radiant floor system be installed. The new system combines a forced air system that uses a fan coil heated by the boiler that also warms the water for the radiant heating. This system maintains the historic integrity of the original floor grilles and also provides radiant heat. Most important, the system provides adequate warmth throughout the cottage during the winter.

This phase of the project was difficult primarily because the original stone floor had to be removed in order to install the radiant heat piping. Bill Martinelli photographed and numbered each flooring stone so that it could be cataloged when removed and reinstalled in its exact original position.

After considerable research, in an effort to reduce the use of plastics on the job, John specified expanded perlite (a volcanic min-

Bill Martinelli volunteered to map and photograph the stone floor prior to removal.

The stone floor was replaced after all mechanical, electrical, and plumbing systems had been trenched and installed in the insulation and concrete slab.

eral) insulation beneath the concrete slab in lieu of the conventional rigid board insulation. The Perlite Association of America donated the perlite and the contractor was pleased to discover that the insulation proved easy to work with. Below- grade electrical conduit and ductwork was trenched through the compacted perlite, which is fire-proof and has an insulation value similar to fiberglass batt insulation. Unlike rigid board, perlite's insulation value does not decrease over time. The four-inch-thick concrete slab on top of the perlite contains the plastic piping for the hot water radiant heating. The flagstones are laid on top of the concrete slab.

The Kohler Company donated plumbing fixtures very similar to the original "desert sand" color specified by Wright. John recommended not installing a prefabricated metal shower stall as specified in the original design due to accessibility problems. This proposed change also led to a long series of discussions with DOA and SHS staff. Eventually, they agreed that the metal stall was not a crucial piece of the design. For the shower, John used insulated stainless steel panels attached directly to the stone walls on two sides, with a shower curtain on a rod attached to the ceiling to fully enclose the shower. A floor drain was set directly into the stone floor. Typically referred to as a European shower, the open plan allows for handicap access. Grab rails which double as towel hangers were installed adjacent to the toilet, and other hardware further accommodates the physically challenged.

INTERIOR FINISHES AND FURNISHINGS

Most preservation projects have a goal of restoring the structure to a specific time in history. Unfortunately the cottage was not complete at the time of Wright's and Peterson's deaths, so the rehabilitation aimed to represent "what might have been." Although the approach is unusual, the SPCC thought it appropriate, in that the cottage would ultimately stand as a tribute to both Wright and Seth Peterson.

In 1989, the cottage interior was completely in ruins. Although wooden elements such as ceiling boards, trim, and cabinetry were damaged beyond repair, enough remained to determine the original dimensions and material used. Careful measurement and documentation of the ruined pieces, combined with the original detailed drawings, enabled exact duplicates to be made. John was particularly pleased to find a coral-colored laminate that matched the original kitchen countertops.

Wright usually designed individual furniture pieces for Usonian homes. He believed ". . . every chair must eventually be designed for the building it is to be used in. Organic architecture calls for this

The severely deteriorated cottage interior in 1989.

chair which will not look like an apparatus but instead be seen as a gracious feature of its environment, which can only be the building itself." *(The Natural House)*

Wright's furniture designs for the cottage include tables, chairs, hassocks, a bed, side table, and built-in settle seating, none of which were ever built. Replica furniture was constructed in accordance with the original plans and specifications. The lack of historic furnishings proved to be an asset, in that the replicas now in the cottage are of little intrinsic value.

Unfortunately, the original drawings did not include designs for dining chairs. Bert Goderstad, a close friend of Peterson's, believes that Seth instructed Wright not to design these components as he had built some of his own. Many preservation architects believe that "new" components such as furniture should be clearly different from historical pieces, so that the building can be properly interpreted. However, others believe the contrast between original and new furniture can disrupt the aesthetics of the project. John agreed with the latter approach and recommended that new chairs be designed to be sympathetic with the other Wright furniture. He spent considerable time researching furniture designed by Wright in the 1950s, and designed two chair types consistent with Wright's designs of this period and the other furniture in the cottage. Upholstery fabric of texture and color similar to that which Wright often used was chosen for the chairs and settle seating.

Newly designed kitchen cabinetry emulates the heavily damaged originals.

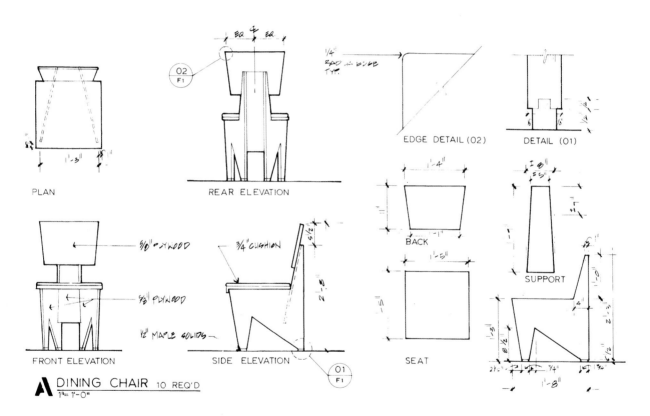

PLAN

REAR ELEVATION

EDGE DETAIL (02)

DETAIL (01)

FRONT ELEVATION

SIDE ELEVATION

BACK

SEAT

SUPPORT

⅜" PLYWOOD

¾" CUSHION

⅜" PLYWOOD

½" MAPLE SOLIDS

▲ DINING CHAIR 10 REQ'D
1" = 1'-0"

Eifler & Associates drew plans for new dining room chairs that complement the furnishings designed by Frank Lloyd Wright for the cottage.

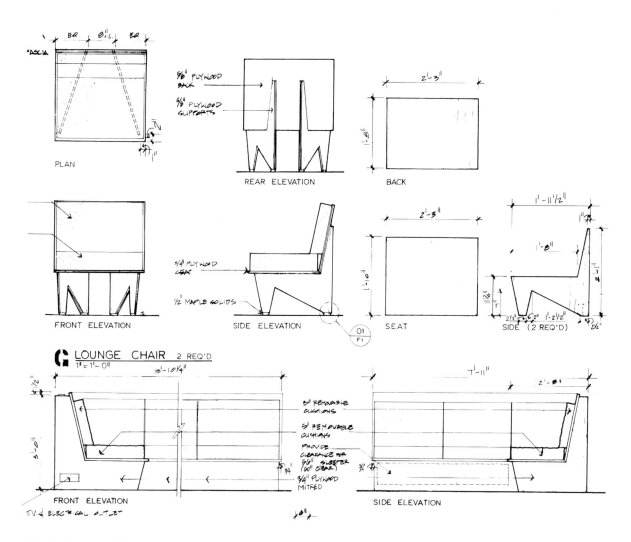

Eifler & Associates' designs for the new living room chairs and settle seating.

SITE WORK

The Seth Peterson Cottage was one of many homes built on Mirror Lake. Although all the other buildings along the lake were removed when the land was purchased for the state park, the ornamental plantings put in by the original owners remained. The state has a nonintervention policy in most state parks to allow nature to achieve its own vegetative balance. When Owen Pritchard lived in the Seth

This mid-1960s photograph clearly shows the strong visual connection between the Seth Peterson Cottage and Mirror Lake.

Landscaping in the mid-1960s.

Peterson Cottage he planted a number of spruce, pine, and cherry trees which appeared foreign to an area characterized by large red and white oaks. Photographs from 1959 and the early 1960s taken from the terrace of the cottage show a spectacular view of Mirror Lake which new growth obscured.

With the assistance of landscape architect Ted Wolff, who has extensive experience restoring historic landscapes, including Graceland Cemetery in Chicago, a plan was developed that removed inappropriate plantings and restored a view corridor to the lake. As the cottage was constructed of materials native to the region and designed to connect the inhabitants with nature, Ted felt that the landscape

The new landscaping included bulldozer work to improve drainage near the cottage.

design should consist primarily of native plants. The restoration of the view corridor was significant for the enjoyment of guests, and even more importantly, it shows why Wright designed and sited the cottage as he did. Rarely does one advocate the removal of trees, but in some cases it is necessary and actually complements the site and the structure.

On a practical level, the cottage required a number of services that could not be hidden, including a well, a large LP gas tank, and storage of off-season furniture, supplies, and equipment. John designed a simple shed that would both screen the large propane tank and provide for necessary services and storage. Constructed of cedar board and batten walls, the shed complements the cottage design by using a similar shed roof, trim, and window details.

New site work included a large capacity LP tank and a newly designed storage shed which echoes the cottage. It is undoubtedly the only storage shed in Wisconsin with mitred-glass windows.

PART 4

THE COTTAGE TODAY

■ ■ ■

The Seth Peterson Cottage seen from the hillside below.

▰ P A R T   4   •   T H E   C O T T A G E   T O D A Y

When the cottage was dedicated in June 1992 interior furnishings were not finished. The furniture had not been completed and a bar sink substituted for the yet-to-arrive kitchen sink. Work continued on the final details, but the cottage welcomed its first overnight guests in July 1992. (The first guests slept on a mattress that arrived 10 minutes before they did.)

Since then, the cottage has been wildly successful. Instead of the hoped-for 36% occupancy—131 days annually—needed to ensure financial stability, the cottage has been occupied more than 325 days

The ribbon-pulling ceremony to dedicate the Seth Peterson Cottage. Left to right: Tom Jeffris, Barbara Elsner, Kermit Traska, Audrey Laatsch, Charles Thompson (representing the governor), and Taliesin architect Tom Casey.

per year for more than four years—a phenomenal 89% occupancy rate. It has received national and international publicity on the ABC television network, in *The New York Times, Architectural Digest*, and *House Beautiful*, as well as much regional publicity. Consequently, it has had guests from as far away as Australia. And many guests return for second, third, and even fourth visits. Because of this enthusiastic reception, the cottage is booked well in advance, with popular weekends and holidays reserved up to two years ahead.

Guests are enchanted. "We stand in awe of every detail. You can't absorb it all at one stay," wrote one. Another offered, "As a student and admirer of FLW for 30+ years, this has been a wonderful experience for me. I am once again moved by the power of principle in the hands of a genius and the magic interplay of intellect and emotion a building such as this affords. . ." One enjoyed the merger of nature and architecture. "It is truly an inspiration to live in a Wright home for even a short period of time. Words cannot describe all that is experienced here, from the scenic views to the feeling of outdoors while sitting by the fire at night. . . ." A winter visitor added, ". . . we sit alone savoring the simple life but feeling so rich. Bare feet on the flagstone floor! Throwing another log on this awesome fireplace! . . . A beautiful Wisconsin snowfall, listening to Strauss, and watching the critters."

The cottage rehabilitation project, and John Eifler and Audrey Laatsch as individuals, have won six awards, from the Wisconsin Association of Historic Preservation Commissions, the State Historical Society of Wisconsin, the Wisconsin Trust for Historic Preservation, the Chicago Chapter of the American Institute of Architects, the Frank Lloyd Wright Building Conservancy, and Wisconsin State Parks.

The popularity of the cottage gives the conservancy financial stability. It has no debts, so all income from the $225 per night rental rate goes toward cottage operations.

Managing the cottage requires keeping detailed financial records because the income goes for a number of different purposes. Major allocations are:

• 30% of the rental rate to the Sand County Service Company, which manages the cottage, handling all reservations and contact with guests, and providing cleaning, linens, minor repairs, and other management services.

• 5% of the rental rate to the Department of Natural Resources according to the terms of the conservancy's 15-year lease agreement. This provides more than $3500 annually to the DNR. (Income from conservancy memberships, merchandise sales, and other donations is not figured into the calculation of the 5% rent to DNR.)

• Payment for on-site operating costs of utilities, routine maintenance, such as snowplowing, firewood, grass cutting, and replacement of household items such as dishes and glassware.

• Payment for off-site services, such as the conservancy's accountant, insurance (the building is insured by the state but the contents are insured by the conservancy; conservancy board members also have a board members liability policy), and membership dues in Wright and historic preservation organizations. The conservancy is a member of the Frank Lloyd Wright Wisconsin Heritage Program, which includes publicity for the cottage in its brochures. The conservancy is also a member of the Wisconsin Dells Visitors and Convention Bureau, the Madison Convention and Visitors Bureau, and the Baraboo Chamber of Commerce. These organizations provide publicity in their promotional materials, and membership gives the conservancy a chance to develop relationships with local businesses.

Volunteers Bill Martinelli and Rich Wandschneider change lightbulbs.

Income remaining after the bills are paid goes into escrow accounts for long-term cottage maintenance and for an eventual rent subsidy for those who cannot afford the standard rate.

The maintenance account has already been used.

The cottage needed a $10,000 cleaning and tuck-pointing job in spring of 1996, and the high occupancy rate has caused serious wear and tear on the furniture and upholstery, resulting in the need to replace some furniture and reupholster many of the cushions. A plan for spreading major costs such as these over a period of years, plus having a reserve to cover unexpected expenses, is key to ensuring that the cottage will be properly maintained in the future.

Even though the income from cottage rental pays all the cottage-related bills, the conservancy continues as a membership organization with annual (or lifetime) dues. Currently, the conservancy has 200-plus members. It sells cottage-related merchandise such as postcards, jewelry, a Wright calendar, books, and T-shirts. Income from membership dues and merchandise sales is used to pay for the conservancy's semi-annual newsletter and for other costs of operating a not-for-profit organization. Some 400 visitors tour the cottage every year during the open houses held the second Sunday of every month from 1:00 to 4:00 p.m. Visitors pay $2 per person.

The conservancy board of directors has changed its role several times since the SPCC was organized in 1989. Originally, the group was concerned with organizing and planning the rehabilitation project. Next, members began fundraising, working with John Eifler in negotiations with the state agencies, and assisting with construction oversight. Now that the rehabilitation project is complete, the board concentrates on marketing and publicity, daily operations and maintenance, and long-term maintenance plans. In addition, board members are the core of cottage volunteers. Much of the work of operating the cottage and the conservancy itself continues to be done by volunteers. They lead tours, do routine maintenance, produce the newsletter, fill merchandise orders, maintain contact with the DNR and the management company, continue fundraising projects, and lead special projects such as the design of a new cottage entry gate.

The current board includes three members—Audrey Laatsch, Bill Martinelli, and Mark Vladick— who were on the original board. Other members of the current board include architects, local business owners, historic preservationists, a publicist, an attorney, and a decorative arts professor. Kermit Traska continues as the Department of Natural Resources liaison to the conservancy.

The Seth Peterson Cottage Conservancy began as a group of concerned citizens who saw the potential of a forgotten work by a master architect. They viewed the cottage not as an eyesore but rather as an integral component of their local history and a part of their community. From enthusiastic but naive beginnings, the SPCC learned how to raise a significant amount of capital and manage a cultural icon using an innovative and profitable approach. If there is a single ingredient to which the Seth Peterson Cottage rehabilitation owed its successful completion, it was the optimistic and determined attitude of Audrey Laatsch and the other members of the Board of Directors of the Seth Peterson Cottage Conservancy, who had the courage and determination to make the rehabilitation a reality. The board developed a carefully considered plan for the rehabilitation and subsequent use of the cottage; a plan that protected the historic integrity of the building while incorporating changes needed to ensure successful operation of the cottage as a vacation rental. Once they had developed a plan, they stuck to their vision through long negotiations with state agencies.

The Seth Peterson Cottage project offers lessons in public-private cooperation, not only to the State of Wisconsin, but to other organizations and individuals interested in preservation. The cottage, for years a white elephant, was transformed into an economically self-sufficient venture. The conservancy agreed to rehabilitate the structure primarily with privately raised money, easing the fears of state officials regarding public expense. In return, the conservancy received state authorization and seed money.

Many states own significant historic structures that need rehabilitation and new utilization strategies. Perhaps these states should reevaluate the current status of those buildings and look toward the private sector to implement programs to preserve publicly owned historic sites. On the other hand, a willing private sector must round out the equation. As of this writing, the states of Wisconsin, Maryland, Virginia, and New York are addressing similar preservation issues regarding state-owned property and private initiatives. The public-private partnership is slowly evolving as a preferred alternative to the limited options available through the public sector alone. Such joint relationships promote the restoration and use of historic buildings, encourage all aspects of historic preservation, and give the public a more direct sense of ownership of our cultural heritage.

The Seth Peterson Cottage rehabilitation presents a well-conceived formula for preservation. Through the efforts of a dedicated group of advocates, an architectural masterwork was saved from inevitable loss.

IN-KIND CONTRIBUTIONS

Ace Well and Drilling
Wisconsin Dells, Wisconsin
Pump and equipment

Automatic Temperature Control
Madison, Wisconsin
Water heater

Banner Arts
Madison, Wisconsin
Banner

Baraboo Screen Printing
Baraboo, Wisconsin
T-shirts and printing

Baraboo Sysco Food Service
Baraboo, Wisconsin
Food for dedication

Tommy Bartlett Enterprises
Wisconsin Dells, Wisconsin
Prints and notecards

Beard Trucking
Wisconsin Dells, Wisconsin
Drayage

Best Service
Reedsburg, Wisconsin
Tablecloths for dedication

Century House
Madison, Wisconsin
Guest book / serving pieces

Chuck's Locksmith
Wisconsin Dells, Wisconsin
Locks and keys

Cutlip Communications
Madison, Wisconsin
Communications consulting

Dells Lumber & Construction
Wisconsin Dells, Wisconsin
Lumber

Dimensions II
Madison, Wisconsin
Dinnerware

Eifler & Associates
Chicago, Illinois
Architectural services

Ray & Hazel Estervig
Madison, Wisconsin
Boat dock

Boris Frank Associates
Verona, Wisconsin
Organizational consultant

General Heating
Madison, Wisconsin
Burnham boiler

Glant
Seattle, Washington
Fabrics

Gretchen Bellinger
New York, New York
Fabrics

Hartje Lumber, Inc.
LaValle, Wisconsin
Plywood

Heatway
Springfield, Missouri
Radiant heating system

Hill's Gallery & Gifts
Baraboo, Wisconsin
Framing

Hoffman House - Janesville
Madison, Wisconsin
Food for fundraising brunch

Holiday Inn
Wisconsin Dells, Wisconsin
Food and dining utensils

Holiday Wholesale
Wisconsin Dells, Wisconsin
Food / supplies

Jerry A. Minnich Assoc.
Madison, Wisconsin
Brochure design

Jimmy's Del-Bar
Lake Delton, Wisconsin
Supplies for dedication

Jung Seed Co.
Randolph, Wisconsin
Grass seed

King Koil
Minneapolis, Minnesota
Mattress

Kinko's
Milwaukee, Wisconsin
Photocopying

The Kohler Company
Kohler, Wisconsin
Bath / kitchen fixtures

Lakes Gas
Reedsburg, Wisconsin
Tank installation

Land's End
Dodgeville, Wisconsin
Bed and bath linens

Lee Jofa
Carlstadt, New Jersey
Fabrics

George Longnecker
Morgantown, West Virginia
Landscape consulting

Lutheran Brotherhood
Hastings, MN, Sauk Co., WI
Dock materials

Marshall Field's
Madison, Wisconsin
Coffee maker

Martin-Marietta Corp.
Rock Springs, Wisconsin
Pink Lady gravel

McGann Furniture
Baraboo, Wisconsin
King Koil mattress

Midwest Perlite Co.
Appleton, Wisconsin
Insulation

Mid-Wisconsin Security, Inc.
Madison, Wisconsin
Security system

Milaeger Landscaping
Racine, Wisconsin
Landscaping design and plants

Olson's Paint & Decorating
Wisconsin Dells, Wisconsin
Framing

Orange Tree Imports
Madison, Wisconsin
Cottage furnishings

Pella Windows
Pella, Iowa
Cottage and storage shed windows

Prange Way
Reedsburg, Wisconsin
Kitchen supplies

Racine Millwork
Racine, Wisconsin
Storage shed siding and millwork

Roberts Construction
Madison, Wisconsin
Construction services

Sand County Service Co.
Lake Delton, Wisconsin
Photocopying

Bruce A. Schultz
Madison, Wisconsin
Legal services

Scott Construction
Lake Delton, Wisconsin
Driveway construction

Alice Seeliger
Oregon, Wisconsin
Newsletter design

Joe Seep Plumbing
Reedsburg, Wisconsin
Topsoil

Richard Steinhorst
Baraboo, Wisconsin
Fireplace grate and wood box

Ken Stevens
Reedsburg, Wisconsin
Legal services

Sub-Zero Freezer Co., Inc.
Madison, Wisconsin
Refrigerator

Sugar River Woodworks, Inc.
Brodhead, Wisconsin
Furniture, cabinetry

Thermador
Los Angeles, California
Cooktop and oven

Thompson's Flowers
Wisconsin Dells, Wisconsin
Flowers

Top Hat
Baraboo, Wisconsin
Chimney repair

Ver Halen, Inc.
Madison, Wisconsin
Window installation, screens

Kristin Visser
Madison, Wisconsin
Writing, editing

Rick Waldschmidt
Oregon, Wisconsin
Framing

Wolff & Associates
Chicago, Illinois
Landscape design

MAJOR FINANCIAL CONTRIBUTORS

The Jeffris Family Foundation

State of Wisconsin - Department of Natural Resources

State Historical Society of Wisconsin

The Andy Warhol Foundation

Tommy Bartlett Enterprises

David and Julie Egger

Fanuc Ltd., Japan

Robert and Patricia Francis

The American Society of Interior Designers, Wisconsin Chapter

Wisconsin Power and Light Company

Pleasant Rowland

American Family Insurance

Firstar Bank - Madison

Eifler & Associates, Architects

Audrey Laatsch

Ishnala Restaurant

Webcrafters - Frautschi Foundation

Mark & Jill Vladick

George L. N. Meyer Family Foundation

Marshall Erdman

And many other contributors from Wisconsin, the United States, Canada, and Japan.

GLOSSARY

Battered— Inclined from the vertical. A wall is said to be battered or to have a batter when it recedes as it rises.

Clerestory— A window, or row of windows, placed high on a wall just below where the wall meets the roof.

Cricket— A sheet of metal or other material used to weatherproof joints and edges, and to channel rainwater away from a chimney or wall.

Furring— The application of thin pieces of wood, brick, or metal to joists, studs, or walls to form an even surface or provide an air space.

Header— A beam fitted over an opening to support joists, rafters, or wall studs.

Joists— Boards laid parallel to each other from wall to wall in a structure to support a floor or ceiling.

Mitred window— Formed by cutting the edges of two pieces of glass at angles and fitting them together.

Parapet— A low wall along the edge of a roof or terrace.

Rise to run— The increase in height in relation to a corresponding increase in distance, i.e. a four-foot rise along a twelve-foot distance is a rise to run of four to twelve.

Scupper— An opening in the wall of a building through which water can drain from a floor or flat roof.

Settle— Bench seating with a high back and storage under the seat.

Wythe— A single thickness of masonry (concrete block, brick, or stone.) The cottage walls are three wythes thick, consisting of a wythe of concrete block between two wythes of sandstone.

PHOTOGRAPH AND ILLUSTRATION CREDITS

p. xiii: photographer unknown

p. 2: Frank Lloyd Wright Foundation

p. 3: The Hiebing Group

p. 4, 5: Frank Lloyd Wright drawings are copyright
© 1996 The Frank Lloyd Wright Foundation

p. 6, 7, 8, 9, 10, 11, 12: photographer unknown

p. 13: Dave Daniels

p. 15: Dave Daniels

p. 16, 18, 19: John Eifler

p. 21: Dave Daniels

p. 26: Robert Queen, WI DNR

p. 28, 29: Eifler & Associates

p. 35: John Eifler

p. 36, 37, 38: Robert Queen, WI DNR

p. 39: Bill Martinelli

p. 41: Bill Martinelli

p. 42: Dave Daniels

p. 43: Bill Martinelli

p. 44, 45, 46, 47: John Eifler

p. 48: Bill Martinelli

p. 49, 50: John Eifler

p. 51, 52, 53: Bill Martinelli

p. 55, 56: John Eifler

p. 57: Eric Urtes

p. 58, 59, 60: John Eifler

p. 61, 62: Eifler & Associates

p. 63, 64: photographer unknown

p. 65: Kristin Visser

p. 66: Bill Martinelli

p. 67: Kristin Visser

p. 69: Robert Queen, WI DNR

p. 71: Kristin Visser

p. 74: Beth Singer, courtesy Pella Windows

Endpapers: Eifler & Associates